Animal Pranksters

Silver Argiope Spiders

by Julie Murray

2

Dash!
LEVELED READERS
An Imprint of Abdo Zoom • abdobooks.com

2 Dash!
LEVELED READERS

Level 1 – Beginning
Short and simple sentences with familiar words or patterns for children who are beginning to understand how letters and sounds go together.

Level 2 – Emerging
Longer words and sentences with more complex language patterns for readers who are practicing common words and letter sounds.

Level 3 – Transitional
More developed language and vocabulary for readers who are becoming more independent.

THIS BOOK CONTAINS
RECYCLED MATERIALS

abdobooks.com

Published by Abdo Zoom, a division of ABDO, PO Box 398166, Minneapolis, Minnesota 55439. Copyright © 2023 by Abdo Consulting Group, Inc. International copyrights reserved in all countries. No part of this book may be reproduced in any form without written permission from the publisher. Dash!™ is a trademark and logo of Abdo Zoom.

Printed in the United States of America, North Mankato, Minnesota.
052022
092022

Photo Credits: Alamy, AP Images, Getty Images, Science Source, Shutterstock
Production Contributors: Kenny Abdo, Jennie Forsberg, Grace Hansen, John Hansen
Design Contributors: Candice Keimig, Neil Klinepier

Library of Congress Control Number: 2021950308

Publisher's Cataloging in Publication Data

Names: Murray, Julie, author.
Title: Silver argiope spiders / by Julie Murray.
Description: Minneapolis, Minnesota : Abdo Zoom, 2023 | Series: Animal pranksters | Includes online resources and index.
Identifiers: ISBN 9781098228361 (lib. bdg.) | ISBN 9781644947630 (pbk.) | ISBN 9781098229207 (ebook) | ISBN 9781098229627 (Read-to-Me ebook)
Subjects: LCSH: Orb-weaving spiders--Juvenile literature. | Arachnids--Juvenile literature. | Spiders--Behavior--Juvenile literature. | Zoology--Juvenile literature.
Classification: DDC 595.4--dc23

Table of Contents

Silver Argiope Spider 4

Reflecting Light 18

More Facts 22

Glossary 23

Index 24

Online Resources 24

Silver Argiope Spider

Silver argiope spiders live in North, Central, and South America.

They can be found in gardens, fields, and forests.

These spiders have dome-shaped bodies. Their heads and **abdomens** are silver. Different colored **spines** cover their bodies and legs.

Silver argiope spiders have long legs. Their legs are orange with dark bands.

Females are larger
than the males.
Females measure 1.3
inches (3.5 cm). Males
are about half that size.

13

Silver argiope spiders spin wheel-shaped webs. Webs can be two feet (0.61 m) wide! The spiders add zig-zag patterns to their webs. This gives extra **stability**.

The web catches **prey**. The spiders bite their prey and **paralyze** it. Then they wrap it in silk. They eat many kinds of insects.

Reflecting Light

A silver argiope spider uses its light-colored body parts to reflect ultraviolet (UV) light. Its silk also reflects UV light! This light attracts **prey**.

The UV light tricks **prey** into thinking the spider is a flower. Once prey touches the web it is too late. They are stuck!

More Facts

- Silver argiope spiders are part of the orb-weaving family of spiders.

- They have two sets of eyes. However, they do not have good eyesight.

- A female often eats the male after **mating**.